We Are Money $mart

written by
Floyd Stokes

illustrated by
Sheena Hisiro

Did you know?

Before the 15th century, banks were not very popular. So, people saved their money in pots and jars that were made of hardened orange clay called pygg. Eventually, people used the pygg clay to make special jars to hold spare change. Over time, this "pygg bank" became "pig bank". Potters who heard the term decided to make a coin-saving money holder in the shape of a pig hence "piggy bank".

This book was made possible in part by a grant from
Pennsylvania Credit Union Foundation

Carrying on the Tradition!

To George-
f.s.

For Chi-
s.h.

Special thanks to Tressimee, Dwayne, Sojourner, Hansini, Maddie, Sammie, Devin, Olivia, and Wade.

Learning how money works
Can be lots of fun
Know when to spend a dollar
Save, invest, and to give away one

A credit union is a financial institution that is owned by its members.

A credit union has a volunteer Board of Directors elected by and from the membership.

Make a simple budget
And keep track of every cent
It's the smart thing to do
So you'll know where it went

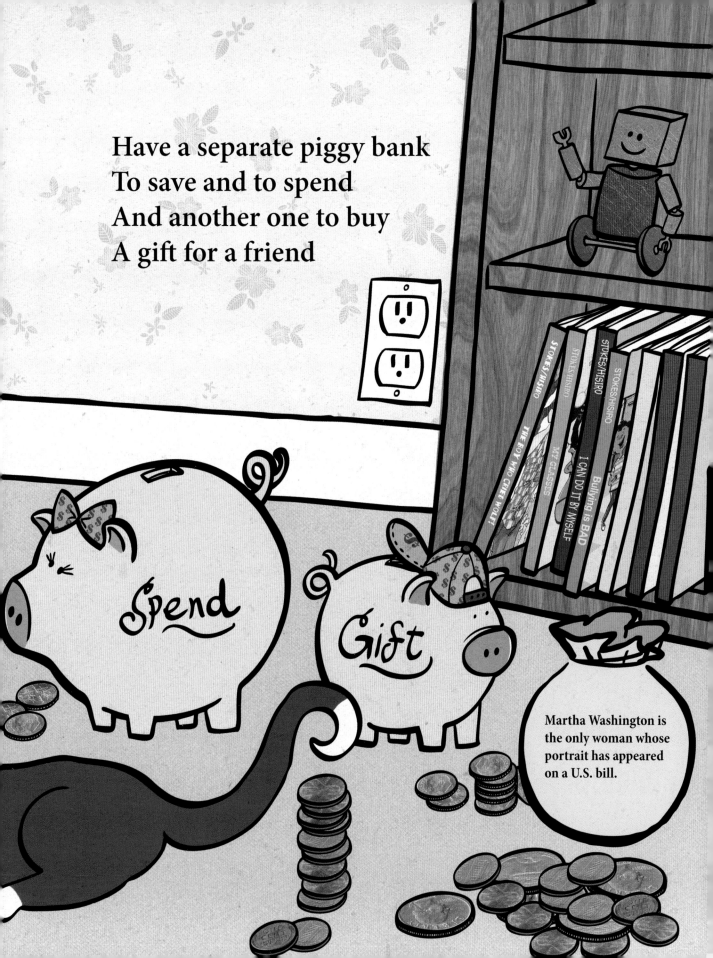

Have a separate piggy bank
To save and to spend
And another one to buy
A gift for a friend

Spend

Gift

Martha Washington is the only woman whose portrait has appeared on a U.S. bill.

Open an account
With your mom or your dad

You can earn lots of money
By doing chores around the house
Like cleaning your room

Credit unions are community-oriented and serve people, not profit.

Mowing the lawn

or feeding the mouse

Working hard for your money
Is the way to go
Being smart with your money
Will earn you lots of dough

The $100 bill has been the largest denomination of currency in circulation since 1969.

Invest your money
And make it work for you
Ten years from now
You will see how much it grew

Invest – to use money to gain value.

Give some money
To help those in need
Some you can buy clothes
And some you can feed

Cattle are the first and oldest form of money and dates back to about 9000 B.C.

You can also buy books
For children to read
When you help others
You do a good deed

When spending your money
Be smart about it
Look for things on sale
So you can save a little bit

IKES

Welcome!
Login or create an account. ✉ Email A Friend

List Price: $99.99
Sale Price: $49.98
Quantity:
1   🛒 Add to Cart   Add to WISH LIST

BIG Savings 50% OFF!

Boys 20 inch Bike

FREE Shipping

Shipping:
Usually ships warehouse in 1-2 business days.

★★★★★   4.8
(127 reviews)

In 1849, the first credit union was organized by Friedrich Wilhelm Raiffeisen in Flammersfeld, Germany.

Don't spend all your money
On drinks and snacks
You can save lots of money
On lunch if you pack

The first U.S. credit union was formed in Manchester, New Hampshire in 1909 with the help of Alphonse Desjardins.

Give, spend, save, and invest
It's the smart thing to do
Continue to learn about money
Your whole life through

Digital cash in the form of bits and bytes will most likely continue to be the currency of the future.

Credit Union Terms

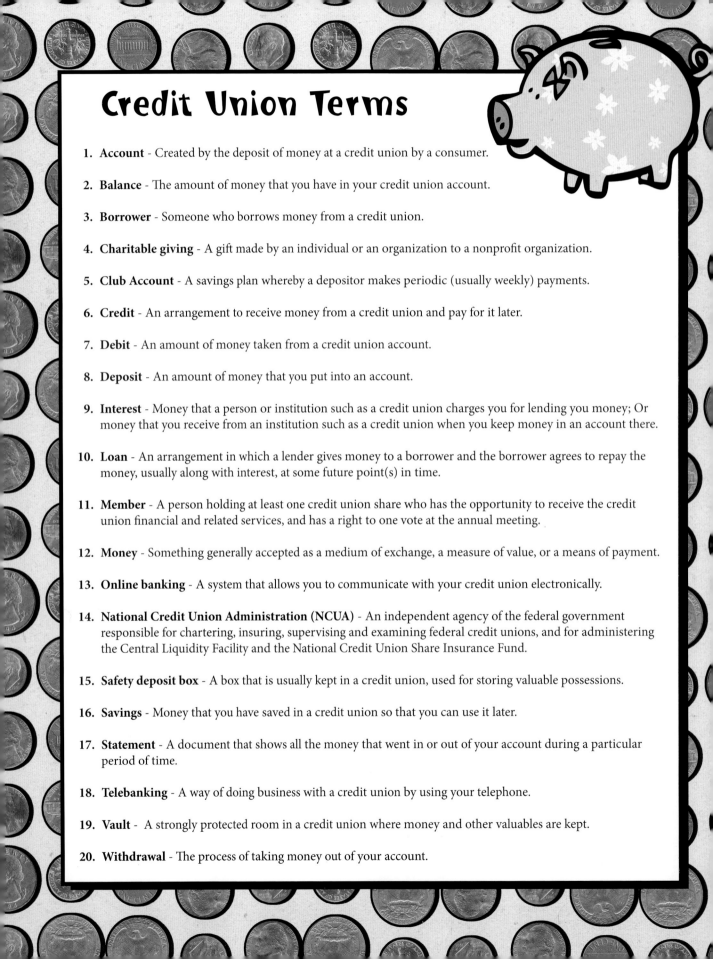

1. **Account** - Created by the deposit of money at a credit union by a consumer.

2. **Balance** - The amount of money that you have in your credit union account.

3. **Borrower** - Someone who borrows money from a credit union.

4. **Charitable giving** - A gift made by an individual or an organization to a nonprofit organization.

5. **Club Account** - A savings plan whereby a depositor makes periodic (usually weekly) payments.

6. **Credit** - An arrangement to receive money from a credit union and pay for it later.

7. **Debit** - An amount of money taken from a credit union account.

8. **Deposit** - An amount of money that you put into an account.

9. **Interest** - Money that a person or institution such as a credit union charges you for lending you money; Or money that you receive from an institution such as a credit union when you keep money in an account there.

10. **Loan** - An arrangement in which a lender gives money to a borrower and the borrower agrees to repay the money, usually along with interest, at some future point(s) in time.

11. **Member** - A person holding at least one credit union share who has the opportunity to receive the credit union financial and related services, and has a right to one vote at the annual meeting.

12. **Money** - Something generally accepted as a medium of exchange, a measure of value, or a means of payment.

13. **Online banking** - A system that allows you to communicate with your credit union electronically.

14. **National Credit Union Administration (NCUA)** - An independent agency of the federal government responsible for chartering, insuring, supervising and examining federal credit unions, and for administering the Central Liquidity Facility and the National Credit Union Share Insurance Fund.

15. **Safety deposit box** - A box that is usually kept in a credit union, used for storing valuable possessions.

16. **Savings** - Money that you have saved in a credit union so that you can use it later.

17. **Statement** - A document that shows all the money that went in or out of your account during a particular period of time.

18. **Telebanking** - A way of doing business with a credit union by using your telephone.

19. **Vault** - A strongly protected room in a credit union where money and other valuables are kept.

20. **Withdrawal** - The process of taking money out of your account.

A publication of the American Literacy Corporation for Young Readers

Text copyright © 2012 by Floyd Stokes.
Illustrations copyright © 2012 by Sheena Hisiro.
Graphic Design by Sheena Hisiro.
First Edition, 2012. Second Edition, 2013. All rights reserved.

ISBN 978-0-9797871-1-9

PRINTED IN CHINA

Floyd Stokes is the founder and Executive Director of the American Literacy Corporation (ALC). He has written eleven books to include: Say Ahh! The Teeth Book, Popcorn, There Was an Old Lady Who Lived in a Shoe, My Glasses, Bullying is Bad, and AJ the Rooster. On May 1, 2009, he was awarded an honorary doctorate of humanities from Central Penn College. In 2010, he read to children in all 50 states.

For more info, visit:
www.superreader.org

Sheena Hisiro has been drawing since she could hold a pencil. She currently lives in Brooklyn, NY, where she is still drawing and loving every minute of it. Sheena has a BFA in Communications Design from Pratt Institute. She has illustrated ten other books including *The Boy Who Cried Wolf!*, *My Glasses, Bullying is BAD, I Can Do It By Myself*, and *Josiah and Julia Go to Church*.

For more info, visit:
oodlesofdoodles.tumblr.com

MIA

HAMM

ROCKS!

MIA HAMM ROCKS!

MIA HAMM ROCKS!
Copyright © Chloe Weber 1999
All rights reserved.
Printed in the United States of America.

Publication of this book is not authorized
or licensed by Mia Hamm, FIFA or the
Women's World Cup organizing committee.

Direct any inquiries to
Welcome Rain Publishers LLC,
532 Laguardia Place, Box 473,
New York, NY 10012.

First Edition: July 1999

1 3 5 7 9 10 8 6 4 2

ISBN   1 - 56649 -176 - 2

Manufactured in the United States of
America by BLAZE I.P.I.

AUTHOR'S NOTE

I am not the world's leading authority on Mia Hamm - but I've been a fan of hers since I played with a #3 ball.

So that's the spirit in which I've written the book, as a sort of appreciation.

Winning

What Phil Knight meant when he said, "There are three athletes who have brought their sports to a new level: Michael Jordan in basketball, Tiger Woods in golf, and Mia Hamm in women's soccer," is that although in sports everyone is in competition, these three are the most determined of anybody to win. They won't allow themselves to lose and they won't allow their teams to lose.

Whenever someone on the team is COMPLETELY determined, the other players have to step up their game because no one wants to let the other players on the team down. If Mia was on your team and working day and night to become a better player, would you feel like skipping practice? Could you have any fun hanging out with your friends if you knew she was out there practicing, and then practicing some more? When someone is that determined, it even makes the opponents better because they don't want to go out on the field in front of a lot of people and let her make them look bad.

Mia played her first game for the US National Team on August 3, 1987 vs. China in Tianjin, China.

She was 15 years old.

In the twelve years since then she has done it all: four national championships at University of North Carolina, first-ever Women's World Cup, first-ever gold medal in women's soccer in the Olympics, scored more than 100 goals and is about to become the all-time leading scorer in international competition, played more games than anybody except Kristine Lilly, even played goalie for a little while against Denmark. She has been in commercials and was chosen as one of the 50 most beautiful people in the world by PEOPLE magazine.

When you come up against the same teams over and over again the way the US national team does, after awhile, they know your moves, and the only way you win games is by improving your skills and doing something new. It is harder to stay the champion than to win the championship in the first place, so the US team has had to work hard all this time to stay on top.

That includes playing when you are hurt, the way Mia did in the Olympics when she made us all proud.

In her book, GO FOR THE GOAL, Mia says that Coach Anson Dorrance of North Carolina once left her a note that said, "The vision of a champion is someone who is bent over, drenched in sweat, at the point of exhaustion when nobody else is watching."

But soccer is a team game so it doesn't matter how good any individual player is unless the team is together.

In soccer - as in basketball - you are only as good as you make the other players on your team. To be a winner, your team has to become like a very big family that does everything together and even thinks together.

I don't know if Mia Hamm is the best player in the world - in fact I don't even think there is such a thing as "the best player in the world" - in soccer, because everyone has a different role.

But I do know that she has given the US a winning tradition based on hard work and unselfish play. You can see she is just as happy to make a pass or corner kick that leads to a goal as to score it herself! She didn't do it alone, but she was a big part of making it happen.

So now wherever girls and women go out and play soccer, we have a great role-model, a woman who decides what she wants and then goes out and gets it. But she doesn't get it by taking all the shots and glory herself. She gets it by passing and sharing and making her teammates winners too!

Photos on the following pages:
Brandi Chastain and Carla Overbeck congratulating Mia Hamm on her
100th career goal.
Mia Hamm after career goal #101.

The University of North Carolina women's soccer team was already a DYNASTY when Mia Hamm and Kristine Lilly arrived in 1989. The Tar Heels had not lost a game since 1985 and had been national champions three years in a row.

In fact, since the National Collegiate Athletic Association (NCAA) began having a national championship for women in soccer in 1982, UNC won in 82, 83, 84, 86, 87 and 88. (Unfortunately George Mason beat them in the Finals in 1985.)

The first superstars were Lauren Gregg, April Heinrichs and Shannon Higgins. They are all now coaches and you can read about them in the section about Coaches later in the book. (But you might want to read about them right now!) They played for pride in front of small crowds most of the time.

North

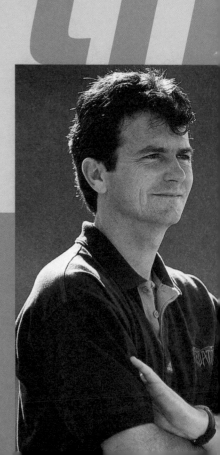

These three were among the true pioneers of women's soccer in the United States. If it were not for them - and Coach Anson Dorrance - it would never have been possible for Mia Hamm to be as good a player or as famous as she is today.

I say that because you can only improve your game by playing with a good team against teams that are also as good as you are - or better. The reason women's soccer is so popular now is because the quality of play is so good. It's fun to watch. American women have their own style just like American men do in basketball. These are areas like jazz and snowboarding where the whole world looks at us and says "WOW."

Coach Dorrance was one of the first people to really understand the difference between men's and women's soccer. He said "there is a genuine team cohesiveness among great women's teams because they have a greater capacity to relate to each other than we do as males."

Coach Dorrance felt that if you want to compete at the top level in soccer, you must have one quality that allows you to dominate the opposition. Whether you are a great athlete, slide tackler, header, can see the field - whatever it is - there has to be one thing you can do that the other team can't stop.

When he first watched Mia Hamm play, "I saw her take a 17-yard run at the ball and I said 'Oh my gosh!' I'd never seen speed like that in the women's game."

So Mia was added to a team that already included Shannon Higgins who had been Player of the Year in 88. (In fact when Shannon Higgins retired from college ball after the 89 season, she had played on four national championship teams and

Carolina

never lost a match with a career record of 89-0-6!) One of the most amazing facts about anybody in championship games in any sport is that Shannon scored the winning goals in the Final Game in 1987, 1988 and 1989!

So as you may already have guessed, UNC won the championship again in 1989 and Shannon Higgins was Player of the Year again. The Final was against Colorado College. After Shannon scored the first goal, Mia assisted on a goal by Kristine Lilly for a 2-0 victory. Carla Werden, who is now Carla Overbeck, captain of the National Team, was an All-American defender.

In 1990, the unthinkable happened - UNC lost a game! After 103 games without a loss, the Tar Heels lost to University of Connecticut 3-2 on penalty kicks. When the Final came, it was UNC vs UConn in a rematch.

Mia made an early run that didn't result in a goal but shook the confidence of UConn. She later scored on a breakaway she created by running through a defender and coming away with the ball. She finished in her usual calm Mia Hamm *style. The final score was 6-0. Kristine Lilly was named Player of the Year and both Kristine and Mia were All-American.*

In 1991, Mia red-shirted so she could train with the National Team for the first-ever Women's World Cup. Red-shirting is what they call it when you take a year off from college competition but still keep that year of eligibility. Kristine Lilly was also on the National Team but instead of red-shirting, she played all the regular season games and then left to go to the World Cup after UNC made it to the Final 4.

Since Coach Dorrance was the coach of the National Team, UNC had to play for the championship without Mia, Kristine and their coach! Assistant Coach Bill Palladino stepped up and so did everyone on the team - especially Tisha Venturini- and UNC defeated University of Wisconsin 3-1. Kristine Lilly was once again named Player of the Year.

Mia was back in 1992. The Final was against Duke under terrible field conditions. UNC's style was to keep the ball on the ground. But with puddles everywhere, the ball kept stopping and players would end up running after their own pass. Everyone was shocked when Duke scored the first goal on a diving header. After almost never having been behind all year, the UNC players were suddenly cold and wet and behind in the Final! Mia responded with a goal that tied the game and Tisha Venturini said "we knew right then we were going to be alright." And they were. Mia scored a hat-trick and UNC triumphed 9-1. Mia was named Player of the Year and Mia, Kristine and Tisha were all All-American.

In 1993 the Final was against George Mason - remember 1985? Kristine Lilly had already graduated but Mia and company had this one under control. Mia assisted from the left and right wings and scored one goal of her own. On one play the tv announcer said "two defenders - not enough." Six different players scored in the game, which ended up 6-0. That made 8 straight championships for UNC and 11 out of 12. Mia was again National Player of the Year.

I bet you're wondering what happened after Mia graduated. During the regular season in 1993, the Tar Heels lost to Duke and tied Notre Dame. They went into the Final game as underdog against Notre Dame. Led by Tisha Venturini who converted from defender to striker, UNC defeated Notre Dame 5-0. Tisha was the new National Player of the Year.

The Men's vs Game

Although soccer is that same game no matter who is playing it, the comparison between men's and women's soccer is very interesting.

Many people feel that men's soccer is much more advanced than women's. Men have been playing soccer at a high competitive level for a very long time. Women's soccer is relatively new to a high level of competition, with only the third Women's World Cup being played this summer. Men have had time to perfect their training, learning what works well to get their bodies into shape. And the more you play against players who are better than you, the more you improve your game.

I will be glad to admit the men's game is more advanced as far as power goes, but the women's game has a much nicer flow to it. Women tend to play the ball much more than men and there is a lot less cheating and fouling, which stops the flow of the men's game. Women also know soccer isn't about how hard you can kick the ball. They try to work together rather than just trying to muscle their way through the game.

The Women's Game

Another extremely important point is that women seem to know soccer is a team game. Everyone has to work together if you want to win the game. Even though one player scores the goal, it is clear that the entire team had to work together to get that goal. Women seem to know each other's play a lot better because they spend more time together as a team. The members of the US national team even live together, and some of the players have been together for up to 12 years.

Soccer is a game that requires mental and emotional as well as physical strength. The game can be won or lost in the blink of an eye and you have to be able to deal with the hardship of losing. Women talk to one another a lot more and are able to help one another out on and off the field. This translates into better teamwork on the field all the time.

As you have probably figured out by now, I strongly favor the way women play soccer over the men's game. That doesn't mean I think women are better than men, I just feel that their style is much nicer and smoother.

1st Women's World

The United States was not supposed to win the first-ever Women's World Cup held in China in 1991.

Several European countries had club teams that were playing ten and more years before women's soccer was even recognized as a varsity sport in college in the United States in 1978.

Since China has more than a billion people to choose from and they were the home team, China had a good chance of winning. Japan had a professional women's league. Norway was a powerhouse.

At 19, Mia was the youngest person on the American team. The reason she red-shirted was that she needed to work full-time to develop her skills. Up to then, Mia was very athletic, really fast and knew how to score goals but she was not a complete soccer player. It was her training in the year leading up to the first World Cup and all the games against tough international opponents that helped Mia become a complete soccer player.

Cup

Coach Dorrance of North Carolina was the National Team coach. Almost half the players on the National Team were from UNC. By selecting so many UNC players for the team, Coach Dorrance knew he had players that understood his system and who had played together already.

Coach Dorrance's system was very offensive-minded. Here on one field he had April Heinrichs, who was captain of the team and went on to become the first woman ever inducted into the Soccer Hall of Fame, Shannon Higgins, Mia Hamm and Kristine Lilly and a couple of weapons he didn't have at UNC: Carin Gabarra and Michelle Akers. On defense he had Carla Werden (now Carla Overbeck, captain of the 1999 World Cup team), Linda Hamilton, Mary Harvey in goal, and 21-year-old Julie Foudy.

If there is really such a thing as "the best player in the world," Michelle Akers was it in 1991. 25 years old and tall at 5'10", Michelle had the most powerful shot in the game and was almost unstoppable on headers. Wherever she went she drew a crowd of people marking her and fouling her.

The Final was played in Guangzhou on November 30. 65,000 fans were there! The opponent was Norway, who had beaten the US team twice in games coming up to the World Cup. The event was sponsored by M&M's.

Pele, the Black Pearl, was there. Considered by many the best man ever to play soccer, his home country Brazil had declared him a "Natural Resource."

Although the American and Chinese governments do not get along, the US players had won over the Chinese fans. The team had scored an average of five goals a game in getting to the Final and the frontline (Carin Gabarra, Michelle Akers and April Heinrichs) had been nicknamed "The Triple-edged Sword." Mia Hamm and Kristine Lilly both played midfield.

Norway dominated the first part of the game until Mia was fouled about 40 yards away from the goal. Michelle walked around the ball as though she was going to take the free kick then circled around the defense. Usually there had been two or three players covering her - but for one moment, there was just one. Shannon Higgins took the kick and Michelle headed it right into the corner of the goal.

The lead didn't last for long though, as Linda Medalen scored a goal for Norway. So at halftime the score was tied.

In the second half Norway was again controlling the play and it looked like just a matter of time until they would score the winning goal. But the American defense held on.

The Chinese fans were doing the wave.

With just two minutes to go before overtime, one of the Norwegian defenders made a weak pass back to the goalie. Michelle Akers saw the pass coming, raced around the defender and got to the ball before the goalie. She moved around the goalie and calmly scored the winning goal in the First Women's World Cup ever!

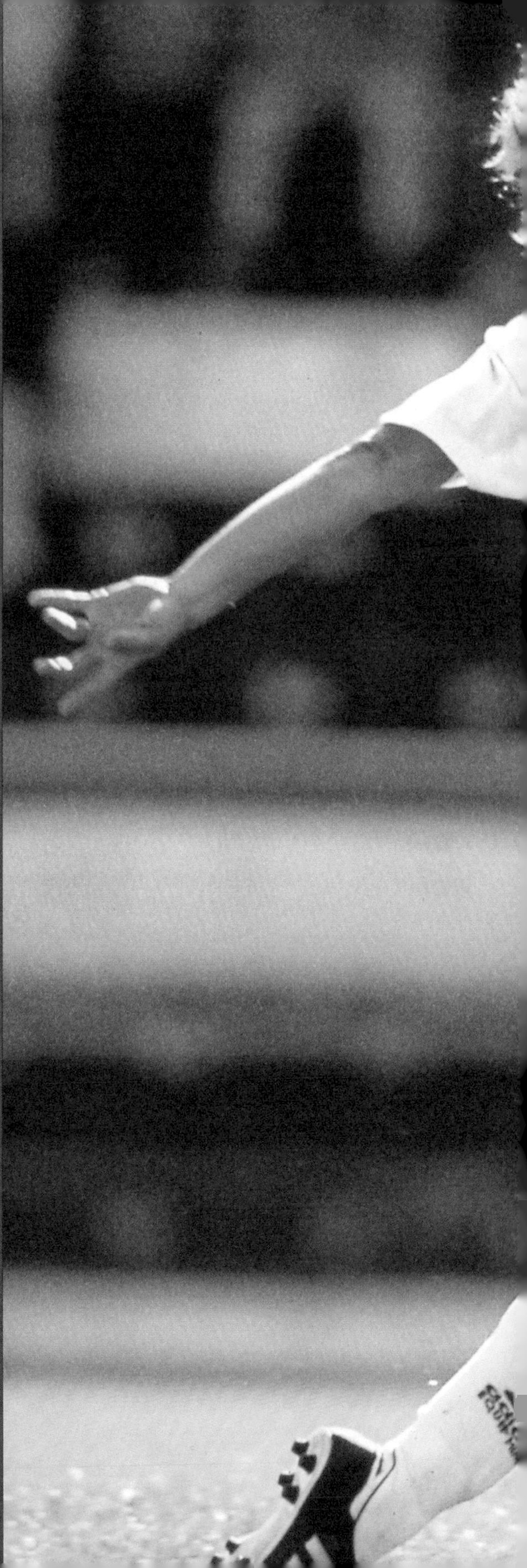

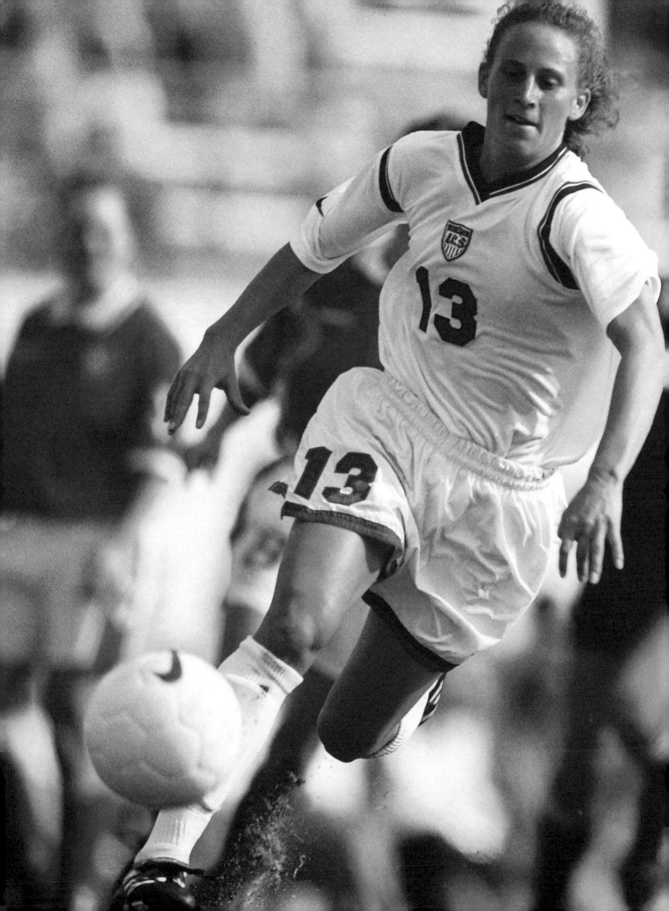

corner&Free Free&kicks

Kristine Lilly scoring on a Mia Hamm corner kick

We have all had games where nothing goes right.

It could be that the ref is not making the right calls or the other team is fouling you or your ankle is killing you or it's too hot, or raining or snowing or the ball doesn't have enough air in it or your coach is trying something new and it's never going to work. You know what I mean.

Top players have these kinds of days too and one of the things I like most about Mia Hamm is that no matter how badly she is hurt or how many times you knock her down, she still gets up and finds a way to get the ball into the net.

I don't know how many assists Mia has gotten on corner kicks but it's a lot, and every time she goes to the corner to take one (left footed or right!), the other team has to be terrified. A corner kick is like a mini game that lasts 5 or 10 seconds. If the offense really has their act together and is in focus, a lot of goals get scored and games are won or lost on corners. Mia is a black belt when it comes to corner kicks.

Another mini game is when you have a free kick close to the other team's goal. You can shoot at the goal, lift it for a header or roll it through for someone else to shoot. The other team might try to form a wall to cut down your angle. They might line up too close to you to make you ask the ref for 10 yards. In the meantime, the rest of their players are marking up. Your team can line up with two players (Mia and Kristine?) over the ball so the other team doesn't know who is going to kick it. A tall defender might sneak up on to the attack. People start running in all directions. And suddenly it's all over. The ball might have sailed over the goal, maybe there was on offside or maybe the ball is in the net. Mia knows how to take advantage of this kind of opportunity.

Another thing I always love to see Mia do is take a throw in. Usually strikers move into scoring position when there is a throw in and let the midfielders come up and take the throw. But sometimes a striker is streaking down the sideline and a defender just barely manages to tap the ball out of bounds. Usually the defender then stops for a second, maybe thinking they've done a good job or maybe they think it's their ball. I don't know how many times I've seen Mia Hamm pick the ball up and throw it over the defender's head to Tiffeny Milbrett or someone else racing up the sideline. Since you can't be offside on a throw in, that player has a breakaway.

Even if the defenders get back and stop the goal, when Mia does something like this, it makes the defenders doubt themselves. Mia has shown she is more into the game than they are and the first time they slip up she is going to take advantage of it. And sometimes the ball just ends up in the goal!

Women's World

The 1994 men's World Cup was held in the United States. As the host country, the American team qualified automatically. Many people hoped that by having the World Cup in the United States, soccer would finally become as popular as baseball or basketball or football - but that didn't happen. Part of the reason it didn't happen is probably because our men's team is not very good. Americans want to see their national team winning and that's exactly what the women's team planned to do when they went to Sweden for the second Women's World Cup in 1995.

It was a different team than the one that won the title in China four years earlier. Anson Dorrance had retired and been replaced by Tony DiCicco as coach. April Heinrichs had retired and was now coaching. Carla Overbeck was the new captain. Michelle Akers was suffering from chronic fatigue syndrome, which meant that sometimes she could play and sometimes she could not. Even when she did play, she was not the dominating player she used to be. Mia was moved up from midfield to striker. Briana Scurry was the new goalie. Tisha Venturini, Tiffany Roberts and Tiffeny Milbrett were now on the team.

In the qualifying round, the US tied China 3-3 in the first game. In their second game against Denmark they were leading 2-0 with two minutes to go when Briana Scurry was ejected. Since the US had already used up all its substitutes, one of the field players had to go into the goal. Who else but Mia? She survived. The US went on to beat Australia 4-1 and advance to the quarter-finals where they beat Japan 4-0.

Their opponent in the semi-finals was Norway. Ever since the US took the world championship away from Norway in 91, the two teams had become bitter rivals. Norway liked to play the long ball and hoped to force the US defenders to make a mistake. They weren't going to let Mia or Michelle Akers beat them again, so they fouled them most of the time.

Cup #2

Michelle had to sit out the three games before Norway with an injured knee. Five minutes into the game Tina Svensson fouled Mia. The next two times Michelle got the ball she was knocked down. Ten minutes into the game, Ann Kristin Aarones scored on a header on a corner kick and Norway was up 1-0.

The offense couldn't get going in the first half. Then with about 15 minutes remaining in the half a really amazing thing happened! The US called time-out! There are no "time-outs" in soccer but in this game there was. What a terrible idea that is. It goes against everything that soccer is about.

Coaches can give players a game plan before the game and make adjustments during halftime and substitutions any time, but while the game is going on it is up to the players to figure out what they need to do. To have time-outs in the Women's World Cup is like saying the players can't figure out what to do by themselves and they need to stop and go over to their coaches who can explain it to them.

Anyway, at halftime Norway had 13 shots, 5 corner kicks and two yellow cards. The US didn't really have one good scoring opportunity. Goalie Briana Scurry had kept them in the game.

In the second half the US substituted Tiffeny Milbrett for Tiffany Roberts to put more pressure on offense. It worked and the US really outplayed Norway - but the ball would not go into the goal. Then with about 15 minutes left, Heidi Store, the captain of Norway, got a red card. So the US had one more player for the rest of the game.

Then we really put the pressure on. Joy Fawcett hit the crossbar twice, Tisha Venturini had some near misses, Michelle Akers had a great cross that Mia almost put in. Briana Scurry made one last save on a break-away by Linda Medalen, but the US just could

not score. You have to give a lot of credit to Benty Nordby, the Norwegian goalie. Finally the whistle blew three times and the announcer said, "It's all over and the USA are world champions no longer."

Norway went on to beat Germany in the Final and the US went against China for third place. Most people only cared that the US was no longer #1, but I think the game against China was very important because it showed that even though they lost to Norway, the US was a team of winners!

The Norwegian coach told reporters he was disappointed in the level of play of the US team during their game, trying to psych the US players out. You already have yourself and your own coaches telling you you could have played better - you don't need the coach from the other team spouting off! I bet the US players still remember that comment.

Anyway, the US had tied China 3-3 in the first game and although this one was not for the championship, it meant a lot to both. Michelle Akers sat out and was replaced by Tiffeny Milbrett. The game was pretty even until the 24th minute when Tisha Venturini headed in a corner kick from Mia. You've probably noticed that Mia takes left corner kicks with her right foot and right corner kicks with her left foot, so the ball is always curving into the goal. This was a left-footer. Briana Scurry made some fantastic saves and that was how the half ended.

China was putting on pressure to tie when in the 55th minute Mia got the ball in mid-field and took off. She blew past the defenders, side-stepped the goalie and put the game away. The announcer could not say enough good things about the goal. He called it absolutely glorious, fabulous, stunning, one of the best of the entire tournament. Mia had a great game and the US took the bronze medal home.

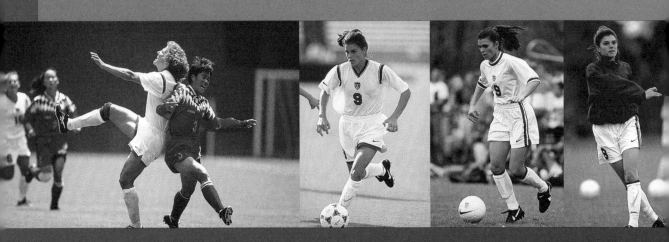

When Mia Hamm was growing up she dreamed about being in the Olympics. In 1996 her dream came true in a bigger and better way than she could ever have imagined! Not only would she get to play in the Olympics, but the Olympics would be in the United States and she would be part of the team to win the first-ever gold medal in women's soccer!

It was exciting for the US National Team to be playing in front of big crowds in China and Sweden but soccer still hadn't caught on in the United States. A lot of people played soccer but not many watched games on tv because the men's team was usually not much fun to watch. But 7 million girls were playing youth soccer and they had a national team full of superstars that they would get to watch as part of the Olympics.

Norway was ranked #1 in the world going into the Olympics because they won the World Cup in 95. The US wanted to regain their #1 ranking - especially in front of their home fans. The two teams met in the semi-final round.

Mia and the US got off to a great start in the first game against Denmark. In front of 25,000 fans, the most ever to see a women's soccer game up till then, Mia had one of her best games ever. She scored one goal, had one assist and was everywhere.

Sweden was the next opponent and they must have watched the game against Denmark. They decided that if they were going to get beat they were going to make sure Mia Hamm did not beat them. They marked her and fouled her all over the place. The US won 2-1 but Mia had to crawl off the field with a badly sprained ankle.

She was hurt so badly she did not play in the third game, against China, that ended up a 0-0 tie. This was a very important game because it meant that the US - and not China - would have to play Norway in the semi-finals.

One of the most important parts of any tournament - and one you usually can't do much about - is the seeds, or ranking. The goal of the seeds is to get the #1 team to play the #2 team in the championship game, to see who really is the best. If #1 meets #2 in an early round and one gets eliminated, the final game won't be as exciting as it could be.

In the Olympics the US did control its own destiny; if we beat China and then China had to play Norway, one of them would have been eliminated and we wouldn't have to play them both. So for Mia to sit out the game against China you know her ankle was REALLY hurting!

Olympic Gold

Many people think the game at the 96 Olympics between the US and Norway was the most important soccer game the US women's team ever played. If they won, they could go for the gold. If they lost, millions of their fans would be disappointed and Norway would still be #1. That is a lot of pressure.

Nothing short of a broken leg was going to keep Mia out of this game.

Norway always plays a very physical game, especially against the US. They had the same strategy as Sweden when it came to Mia. Whenever the ball came in her direction WHAM, one or two of the players from Norway would knock her down.

Eighteen minutes into the game Norway scored. The score stayed 1-0 all through the first half and until there were only 12 minutes left in the game. The pressure was really on! Mia charged into the Norway penalty box with the ball and got knocked down once again. The ref had had enough and awarded the US a penalty kick. Dear reader, I don't know if you would want to take that penalty kick but I sure wouldn't!

Michelle Akers did - and calmly blasted the ball into the back of the net.

The game ended 1-1 and went into overtime.

Ten minutes into overtime Julie Foudy made a great pass to Shannon MacMillan who scored. It was probably the most important goal in the history of US women's soccer and the US advanced into the Final against China.

The Final was played in front of 76,481 fans in Athens, Georgia. That was the most people ever to watch a women's sporting event.

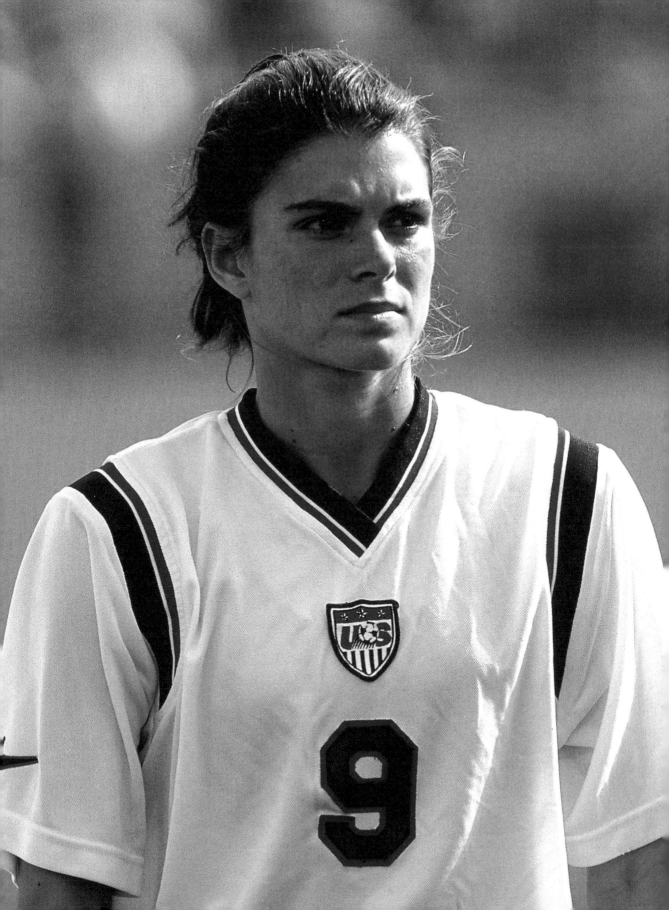

Mia was playing hurt, but just about two minutes into the game she made a great run and blasted the ball over the net from about 25 yards out. Although she didn't score, she gave the Chinese defenders something to think about.

After thinking for about five minutes, Huilin Xie knocked Mia down the next time she got the ball and got a yellow card. Then Kristine Lilly got a yellow card. Sometimes you just have to get a yellow card to let the other team know they can't beat up on you - or Mia!

Michelle Akers was at center-mid with Tiffeny Milbrett and Shannon MacMillan up front with Mia.

About eighteen minutes into the game, Michelle Akers made a long pass to Kristine Lilly who was streaking down the left sideline. Kristine dribbled the ball all the way down into the corner and sent a beautiful cross to the far post. Running full speed, Mia blasted the ball toward the goal before it even hit the ground. (Which is not easy if you've ever tried it!) Han Gao, the Chinese goalie made a great diving save and deflected the ball enough for it to hit the goal post. But it bounced back onto the field where Shannon MacMillan was waiting patiently to be a hero again and put the US ahead 1-0.

1-0 seemed like a comfortable lead until Wen Sun got a breakaway in the 32nd minute and made a beautiful chip shot over Briana Scurry's head to tie the game up. So at halftime it was 1-1.

With only 22 minutes to go in the game, Mia came back to midfield to get the ball and then passed it to a spot on the sideline where Joy Fawcett was going. She got there first and had a breakaway. Joy dribbled down into the corner and then when the defenders came over to stop her, rolled the ball across the goal mouth. Tiffeny Milbrett scored it and did a great somersault to celebrate!

The US shut down China for the rest of the game, although with one minute to go Mia's ankle gave out and she had to be carried from the field.

The US won the gold medal 2-1.

And they won it because they played so well together as a team. In soccer, scoring a goal is also called "finishing." The goals Tiffeny and Shannon finished got started in midfield by Michelle and Mia. They were developed by Kristine and Joy. So, in a way these were both "team" goals.

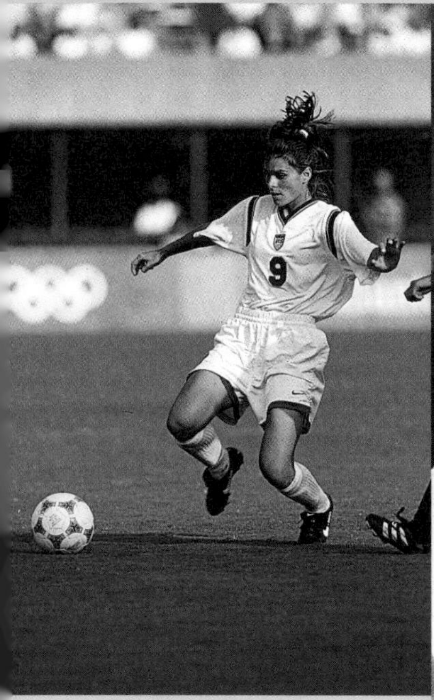
9

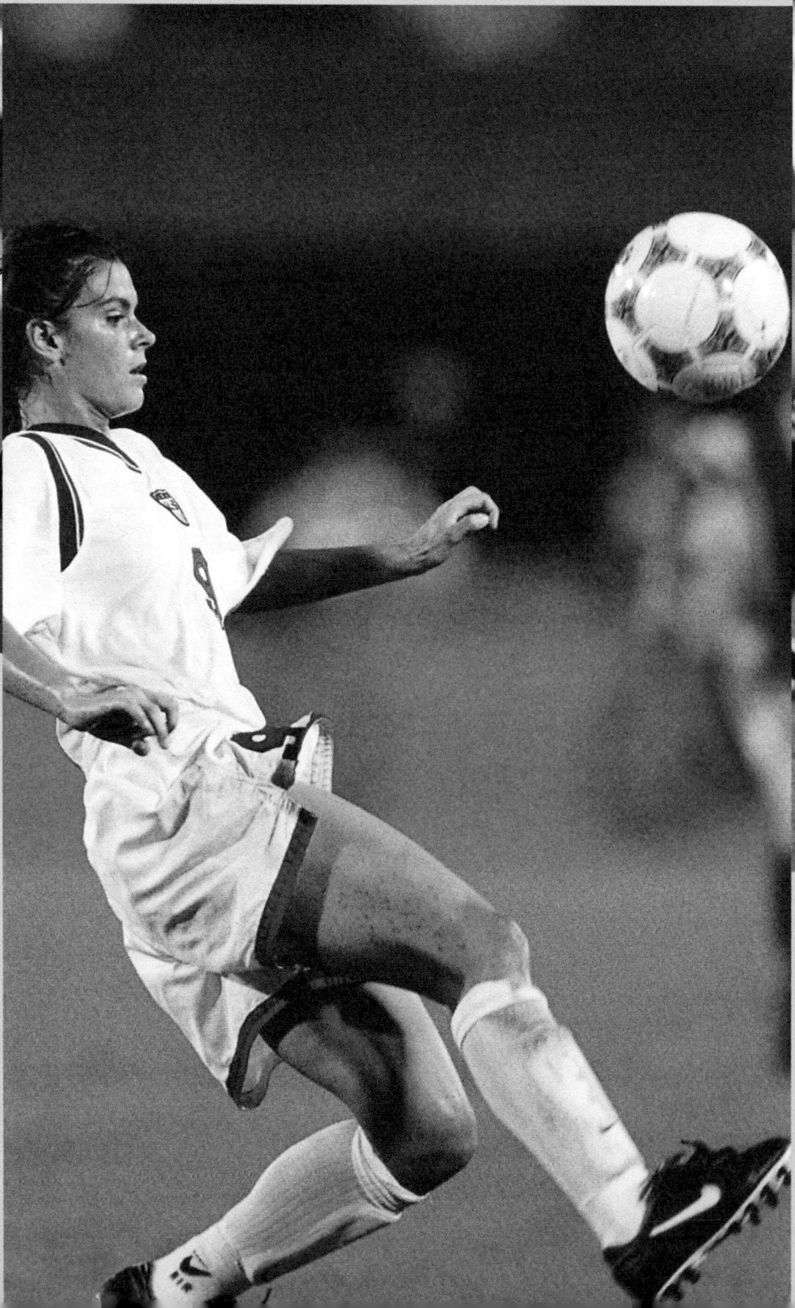

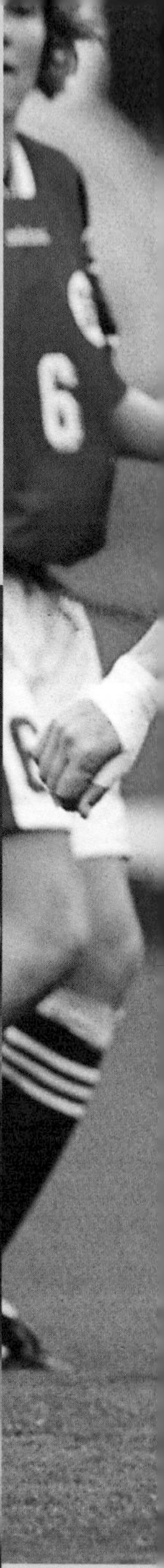
6

A Natural Beauty

In 1997, People *magazine named Mia Hamm* "one of the 50 most beautiful people in the world."

Her teammates teased Mia quite a bit about her selection to the list, but they were proud a soccer player made it.

While most of the people on that list were spending their time working at being beautiful, Mia was practicing or playing soccer.

By putting her on the list, People magazine was saying you can be an athletic woman, compete hard, not spend a lot of time on your hair or makeup, and still be beautiful.

1999 FIFA WOMEN'S WORLD CUP JUNE 19 – JULY 10, 1999

The Official Poster for the 1999 FIFA Women's World Cup was designed by 16-year-old Daphne Yap.

3rd Women's World Cup

I am writing this before the Third Women's World Cup and you are probably reading it while the Cup is going on or after it is over.

Mia and Julie have been in commercials, magazines and the news every night. They will probably be happy to get onto a soccer field and play some games!

Norway, China, Germany and Brazil are trying to spoil the party because if the US wins at home, more and more girls will want to play and our team will continue to dominate. There might even be a women's professional league. If they win, they will go home heroes.

Linda Medalen of Norway said, "It's fun to beat the Americans because they get so upset, make so much noise, when they lose. This is a problem. Never be weak." China and Brazil have improved a lot, and look out for Germany, who got the Silver Medal in the 95 Cup!

For the US, it might be time for Tiffeny Milbrett or Cindy Parlow to step up. In her book, GO FOR THE GOAL, Mia Hamm says Kristine Lilly gets her vote for "the best in the world." Maybe Kristine or Michelle Akers, who is now playing midfield - will come through.

Here are coaches and players - past, present and future-superstars - who will try to win back the Cup for us and, win or lose, will make us proud of them and proud to be women in America in 1999.

Head Coach, U.S. Women's National Team. Hometown: Wethersfield, Connecticut.

Assistant Coach; also Head Coach for the U.S. Under-16 Girls' National Team. Born in Littleton, Colorado. Hometown: Charlottesville, Virginia.

TonyDiCicco

Tony is the third head coach in the history of the national team. He took over the helm in 1994, replacing Anson Dorrance, and has led the team to the first-ever gold medal in Olympic women's soccer (1996) and a third-place finish in the second Women's World Cup in Sweden (1995).

AprilHeinrichs

April was the captain of the 1991 U.S. team that won the first-ever Women's World Cup in China. April, Michele Akers and Carin Gabarra were called "the triple-edged sword" during that tournament. She was U.S. Soccer Female Athlete of the Year in 1986 & 1989 and was voted female player of the 80's by Soccer America magazine. She played collegiate soccer at University of North Carolina where she was named All-American three times. During her four years there, UNC won three NCAA championships and finished as runner-up once. She completed her college career as the all-time NCAA leader in points scored with 225 (87 goals and 51 assists), a record later broken by Mia Hamm and then this past season by Danielle Fotopoulos. UNC compiled a record of 85-3-2 during her years there. In 1998, April Heinrichs became the first female player inducted into the U.S. Soccer Hall of Fame in Oneonta, New York.

Lauren Gregg

Assistant Coach (since 1989); also Head Coach for the U.S. Under-21 Women's National Team. Born in Rochester, Minnesota. Hometown: Wellesley, Massachusetts.

While she was head coach of women's soccer at University of Virginia (until the end of the 1995 season), Lauren's teams had seven consecutive NCAA bids. She was named NSCAA Coach of the Year in 1990 - the only woman ever to receive that honor. An accomplished speaker and clinician, Lauren was listed in the 1997 Who's Who in Women of the World *selected by the International Biographical Center in Cambridge, England.*

Shannon Cirovski

(formerly Shannon Higgins), Head Coach, U.S. Under-18 Women's National Team. Born in Seattle, Washington. Hometown: Columbia, Maryland.

Shannon has excelled at every level of soccer in the United States. During her four-year reign at North Carolina, the Tar Heels won four national championships and never lost a match, compiling a record of 89-0-6! Shannon scored the game-winning goals in the 1987, 88 and 89 championship games. She was Player of the Year in 1988 and 89. She is one of only five players to have her jersey number (#3) retired by the University of North Carolina. As center-midfielder of the national team, Shannon assisted on both goals in the USA's 2-1 triumph over Norway to win the first-ever Women's World Cup in 1991.

Jay Hoffman

Assistant Coach, U.S. Women's National Team. Hometown: Chagrin Falls, Ohio.

Jay is in his second year as Assistant Coach. Before joining the Women's National Team, he was head coach for the U.S. Men's Under-20 National Team.

Kristine Lilly

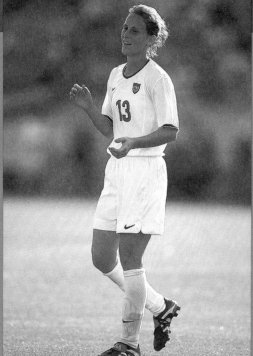

Forward, height 5'4", weight 125. Born July 22, 1971 in New York, NY. Hometown: Wilton, Connecticut. College: UNC.

Kristine is the most-capped player in the history of women's soccer (that means she has played in more international games than anyone else).

She was NSCAA First-team All-American all four of her years at UNC and UNC's Athlete of the Year her senior year. Her UNC jersey number 15 was retired. She was named U.S. Soccer's 1993 Female Athlete of the Year. Widely considered the best flank midfielder in the world, Kristine has scored 66 goals for the national team and has a golden retriever named Molson. The road sign entering her town reads "Welcome to Wilton - Hometown of Kristine Lilly."

Julie Foudy

Midfielder, height 5'6", weight 130. Born January 23, 1971 in San Diego, California. Hometown: Mission Viejo, CA. College: Stanford University.

Only Kristine Lilly and Mia Hamm have more caps for the American team than Julie Foudy. She is the co-captain of the team and an 11-year veteran. A four-time All-American while at Stanford, Julie was Soccer America's Freshman of the Year (1989) and Player of the Year (1991).

Julie's color commentary on ESPN'S coverage of the (Men's) World Cup in France in 1998 won rave reviews everywhere from TV Guide to Sports Illustrated. In March 1997, she travelled to Pakistan to see for herself whether child labor was involved in the making of soccer balls; she also won the FIFA Fair Play Award for that year - making her both the first woman and first American ever to win it.

Carla Overbeck

Defender, height 5'7", weight 125. Born May 9, 1968 in Pasadena, California. Hometown: Dallas, Texas. College: UNC.

Carla is the captain of the U.S. Women's National Team. During her four years at UNC, the Tar Heels won four NCAA championships and Carla was named NSCAA All-American three times. She started every game in the 91 World Cup and was one of only two players to play every minute of the 95 Cup in Sweden (Joy Fawcett was the other). At one point, Carla had played 3,547 consecutive minutes against 19 different national teams, in seven different countries. Her consecutive game streak ended after the 96 Olympics when she took time off to have her son, Jackson August.

Carla is shown in this photo with Carin Gabarra (who is retired now) at Sanford Stadium in Athens, Georgia, after the United States defeated China 2-1 to win the first-ever Gold Medal in Women's Soccer.

U.S. Women's National Team All-Time Goal Scorers (Players with 10 or more goals)

1.	Mia Hamm	104
2.	Michelle Akers	100
3.	Kristine Lilly	66
4.	Carin Gabrarra	53
5.	Tiffeney Milbrett	47
6.	April Heinrichs	38
	Tisha Venturini	38
8.	Julie Foudy	27
9.	Joy Fawcett	18
	Debbie Keller	18
11.	Brandi Chastain	17
	Cindy Parlow	17
13.	Shannon MacMillan	16
14.	Wendy Gebauer	10

Midfielder, height 5'10", weight 150. Born February 1, 1966 in Santa Clara, California. Hometown: Orlando, Florida. College: University of Central Florida.

Michelle Akers

For many years, Michelle has been regarded as one of the finest players in the game. She was the leading scorer in the 91 Cup in China with 10 goals to win the Golden Boot Award.
While at UCF, Michelle was All-American four times; won the first Hermann Trophy and had her jersey number (#10) retired.
A 14-year veteran of the U.S. national team, Michelle has been there from the inception of the program. She was U.S. Soccer's Female Athlete of the Year in 1990 and 91 and is the only person beside Mia Hamm to score 100 goals for the American side in international competition.

On June 7, 1997, she received FIFA's highest honor, the FIFA Order of Merit, at the XVth FIFA Congress in Paris.
Michelle had to take a break from the game after the Olympic Final in 1996, to recover from knee surgery and Chronic Fatigue Syndrome. She has written a book titled *Standing Fast,* which chronicles her battle to overcome CFS and return to a top competitive level.
She has an Arabian horse named Vinnie.

Joy Fawcett

Defender, height 5'5", weight 130. Born February 8, 1968 in Inglewood, California. Hometown: Huntington Beach, California. College: University of California, Berkeley.

Joy was a three-time All-American while at UC Berkeley, where she is still the all-time scoring leader. She was U.S. Soccer's Female Athlete of the Year in 1988 and part of the 91 World Cup Championship team. In 1998, Joy was named MVP of the NIKE U.S. Women's Cup - the first defender ever to win that award. She is one of only nine players to have played in 100 or more international games for the national team. She was also the first women's soccer coach at UCLA, where she was Pac-10 Coach of the Year in 1997. At one point in 97, she was coaching at UCLA, coaching a youth soccer club team and playing for the national team - while raising two children, all at the same time, earning her the title of Ultimate Soccer Mom!

Midfielder, height 5'6", weight 125. Born March 3, 1973 in Modesto, California, which is where she still lives. College: University of North Carolina.

Tisha Venturini

While at UNC from 1991-94, Tisha played on four NCAA championship teams, was Soccer America's Freshman of the Year and NSCAA All-American four times. In 91, she was named the NCAA tournament's Most Valuable Defensive Player. In 94, she was named the NCAA tournament's Most Valuable Offensive Player. She also won the Hermann Trophy that year.

Tisha is the second highest scoring midfielder in the history of the U.S. National Team.

Tiffeny Milbrett

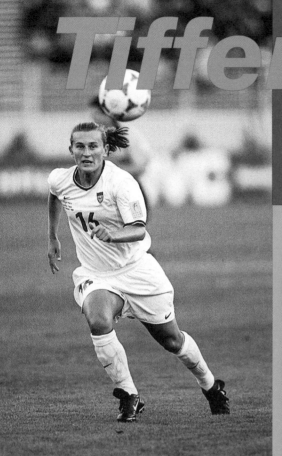

Forward, height 5'2", weight 130. Born October 23, 1972 in Portland, Oregon, where she still lives. College: University of Portland.

Tiffeny scored 103 goals while attending the University of Portland and was tied with Mia Hamm as the NCAA Division I all-time leading goal scorer until their record was broken in 1998 by Danielle Fotopoulos. She was Soccer America's Freshman of the Year and NSCAA All-American three times.

In 1998 Tiffeny scored 14 goals and had nine assists for the national team, finishing second in scoring after Mia Hamm for the third consecutive year.

She scored two goals in the Olympic games, including the game-winner in the Final against China.

Brandi Chastain

Defender, height 5'7", weight 130. Born July 21, 1968 in San Jose, California, and still lives there. College: Santa Clara University.

Brandi attended UC Berkeley in 1986 where she teamed up with Joy Fawcett and was named Soccer America's Freshman of the Year. While at Santa Clara, she led the Broncos to two Final Four appearances and was named NSCAA All-American in 1990.

A forward her entire youth, college and national team career, Brandi converted to defender in 1996 and earned a starting spot on the Olympic team. During 1999, she will become the 10th U.S. player to reach 100 caps.

Her throw-ins are more dangerous than most people's corner kicks! Brandi enjoys snowboarding, visiting pet shelters and teaching herself new languages.

Briana *Scurry*

Goalkeeper, height 5'8", weight 150.
Born September 7, 1971 in Minneapolis, Minnesota. Hometown:
Dayton, Minnesota. College: University of Massachusetts.
Briana has been the USA's #1 goalkeeper since 1994.

Briana has been the USA's #1 goalkeeper since 1994.
She helped UMass to a Final Four appearance in 1993, when she was the
consensus top college keeper. During her college career, Briana recorded
37 shutouts in 65 starts and allowed 0.48 goals per game.

Briana is active in volunteer work for AIDS awareness and research and
with the Make a Wish Foundation. She promised to "run naked through
the streets of Athens, Georgia" if the U.S. won the gold medal in the 1996
Olympics, and did. She has a tattoo of a black panther on her shoulder.

Tiffany Roberts

Midfielder, height 5'4", weight 112. Born May 5, 1977 in Petaluma, California. Hometown: San Ramon, California. College: University of North Carolina.

Tiffany joined the national team when she was sixteen in 1994. She was also California High School Player of the Year in 94. A top track athlete in high school, Tiffany was ranked in the top-20 in the 400 meter dash.

In the 96 Olympics, her defensive play at midfield was a key to the victory over Norway in the semi-finals. Tiffany enjoys playing the piano, dancing and singing.

Shannon MacMillan

Forward, height 5'5", weight 130. Born October 7, 1974 in Syosset, New York. Hometown: Escondido, California. College: University of Portland.

A four-time All-American, Shannon was the 1995 Soccer Player of the Year, as well as winner of the Hermann Trophy as college soccer's best player. In 1996 and 97, she played in the Japanese professional league for Shiroki Serena with college and national teammate Tiffeny Milbrett.

During the Olympics, Shannon led the U.S. team with three goals, including the match-winners against Sweden and Norway. Her "Golden Goal" against Norway was one of the most important in U.S. soccer history, putting the USA into the Olympic Final and avenging the loss at the 1995 FIFA World Cup. Shannon enjoys reading, shopping, playing board games and playing with Joy Fawcett's two daughters.

Cindy Parlow

Forward. height 5'11", weight 145. Born May 8, 1978 in Memphis, Tennessee, where she still lives. College: UNC

Cindy is tied with Danielle Fotopoulos for tallest player on the national team.

The consensus top player in college in 1998, Cindy won both the Hermann Trophy and the MAC Player of the Year Award, joining Mia Hamm as the only two-time winners of both awards. She was Soccer America's Freshman of the Year in 1995 and has been NSCAA All-American all four years at UNC.

Cindy scored the game-winning goal in the champi-onship game of U.S. Women's Cup 97, heading in a cross from Kristine Lilly in the 2-0 win over Italy. She was the youngest member of the Olympic gold-medal winning team in 96 and is already among the top ten goal scorers in U.S. national team history.

Cindy is active in volunteer work at a preschool for underprivileged kids in the Chapel Hill area. She en-joys golf and rollerblading.

Christie
Pearce

Defender, height 5'6", weight 140. Born on June 24, 1975 in Broward County, Florida. Hometown: Point Pleasant, New Jersey. College: Monmouth University.

Christie is an versatile athlete. In high school, she was all-league in basketball, soccer and field hockey. As a senior, she led the Shore Conference in scoring in all three sports.

Christie converted to defense and became a starter for the national team in 1997. She has volunteered as a middle-school soccer and basketball coach and is a talented seamstress - she made her own prom dress.

Lorrie
Fair

Defender, height 5'3" weight 125. Born August 5, 1978 in Los Altos, California, where she still lives. College: UNC.

Lorrie still has one season of eligibility at UNC. In 1998, she was NSCAA All-American. Regarded by many as the top recruit in the country at the end of her high school career (where she also ran track), Lorrie played a major role in helping UNC to national championships in 1996, 97 and a Final appearance in 98. She has been a member of the ACC Academic Honor Role all three years.

A veteran of the U-20 team, Lorrie played in the last four Nordic Cups.She had a breakthrough with the national team in 98, playing in 15 games. Her hobbies include snowboarding, playing the piano and lounging, volleyball and mountain biking.

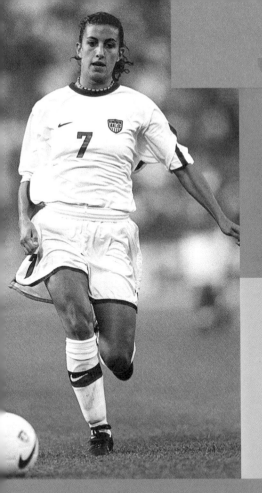

Sara
Whalen

Defender/Midfielder, height 5'6", weight 130. Born April 28, 1976 in Natick, Massachusetts. Hometown: Greenlawn, New York. College: University of Connecticut. Sara was the 1997 Soccer America Player of the Year.

While in high school, She won four letters in track and three in basketball. At UConn, she was NSCAA All-American in 1995, 96 and 97 and scored both goals in the 97 NCAA Final Four semi-final match against Notre Dame, which UConn won 2-1 in one of the biggest upsets in the history of NCAA women's soccer. Sara played in 17 games for the U.S. National team in 1998.

Sarah
Raffanelli

Saskia Webber

Goalkeeper, height 5'9", weight 145. Born June 13, 1971 in Princeton, New Jersey, which is where she still lives. College: Rutgers University.

A four-year starter at Rutgers from 1989-92, Saskia still holds career records for shutouts (32) and saves (413). She was First Team NSCAA All-American as a senior and won the Sonny Werblin Award, the highest athletic honor at Rutgers. Saskia was the USA's starting goalie for most of 1993 and played one match in the 95 World Cup, a 4-1 victory over Australia. She won the Ms. Rutgers bodybuilding contest in 1992 and is an aspiring big wave surfer.

Tracy Ducar

Goalkeeper, height 5'7", weight 140. Born June 18, 1973 in Lawrence, Massachusetts. Hometown: North Andover, MA. College: University of North Carolina.

Tracy had 13 shutouts and a 0.39 goals against average during the regular season in 1995, as the Tar Heels went 23-0-0.

She played in six matches for the national team in 1998 and was a member of the team that won the gold medal at the Goodwill Games. Tracy is active with the "Smoke Free Kids" program, an avid back-packer, snowboarder and rock climber.

Laurie Schwoy

Midfielder, height 5'6", weight 125. Born February 14, 1978 in Baltimore, Maryland, where she still lives. College: UNC.

Laurie still has one season of eligibility at UNC. The premier freshman in the country in 1996, she was Soccer America's Freshman of the Year. The year before, she was the top high school player in the country while a senior at McDonogh in Baltimore, where she was also active in softball, baseball and track and field.

One of the top players on the U.S. Under-20 team, Laurie's midfield play was a key factor in winning the 97 Nordic Cup. She wants to open up her own chain of health clubs someday.

Holly Manthei

Danielle Fotopoulos

Forward, height 5'11", weight 165.
Born March 24, 1976 in Camp Hill,
Pennsylvania. Hometown:
Altamonte Springs, Florida.
College: University of Florida.

Danielle is the all-time leading scorer in the history
of college soccer, having shattered the record
held by Tiffeny Milbrett and Mia Hamm with an
amazing 118 career goals.

In 1998 she finished a storybook year by leading
Florida to the NCAA championship and scoring
the winning goal on a free kick in a 1-0 upset of
North Carolina.

While at Lyman High School in Orlando, Danielle
competed in six sports, lettering in soccer, swim-
ming, tennis, cross country, track & field and basketball.

During 1997, she suffered a serious knee injury
She has recovered and rejoined the national team.

Susan Bush

Forward, from St. John's High
School in Houston, Texas. Born on
November 10, 1980, Susan is the
youngest player on the residency
roster. She has verbally committed
to attend UNC.

Michelle French

Defender, University of Portland. A four-year starter at Portland and NSCAA First-Team All-American as a senior, Michelle collects match books.

Jen Grubb

Defender, University of Notre Dame. A three-time NSCAA All-American, Jen still has one year of eligibility at Notre Dame. She played on the Under-20 Nordic Cup teams in 1996, 97 and 98. She likes to write poetry and jet ski.

Siri Mullinix

Goalkeeper, UNC. A three-year starter at UNC, Siri played on two national championship teams. While a senior, she allowed just 7 goals and had 16 shutouts. Siri has played for both the Under-16 and Under-20 national teams.

Kate Sobrero

Defender, University of Notre Dame. A four-year starter at Notre Dame, Kate was NSCAA All-American three-times. She broke her jaw in a collision with Tracy Ducar and had to have it wired for six weeks before returning to play in the Goodwill Games.

Aly Wagner

Midfielder, Santa Clara University. A former Gatorade National High School Player of the Year, Aly played for the Under-16 National Team in 1997 and the Under-21's in 1998. Has had surgery on both knees.

Mia Hamm

Mia Hamm, Forward, height 5'5", weight 125. Born on March 17, 1972 in Selma, Alabama. Hometown: Chapel Hill, North Carolina. College: University of North Carolina.

A two-time winner of the Missouri Athletic Club and Hermann Award (1992 and 93) and three-time NSCAA All-American, Mia played on four NCAA championship teams while at UNC, in 1989, 90, 91 and 92. She completed her collegiate career as the ACC's all-time leading scorer with 103 goals and 72 assists for a total of 278 points. Her UNC jersey number (#19) was retired.

She played her first game for the national team on August 3, 1987 vs China in Tianjin, China, at the age of 15 and was still the youngest member of the team when she played in the 1991 Women's World Cup at age 19.

She is the third player ever to score 100 or more goals in international competition and is closing in on the all-time record of 108 held by Elisabetta Vignotto of Italy. Mia is also the team record holder in career assists with 77 through the end of the 1998 season. She has played more international games than everyone except teammate Kristine Lilly.

She was named U.S. Soccer's Female Athlete of the Year five consecutive years - from 1994-98.

She was part of the first-ever Olympic gold medal winning team in women's soccer and even played goalie against Denmark for a while in the 95 World Cup in Sweden when Briana Scurry was ejected and the United States had used all its substitutes.

Chloe Weber has been playing organized soccer since she was four - with AYSO, MS 51 (Brooklyn), Gjoa, the Elmont Royals and Stuyvesant High School in Manhattan, where she was named first-team All-City as a freshman. She plays center-mid.

Special thanks to Justin Weiss of Allsport for finding so many great photos; to Gina Davis of the Women's World Cup Organizing Committee for the information about other team members, and to James Tung, of Eric Baker Design Associates, whose design rocks! Also my parents and brother, my coaches and teammates on both my soccer teams, RDG, TTH, EESC and Robin Kachka, one amazing soccer player!